STARTERS
MATHS

Playground
Maths

Macdonald Educational

The children are in the playground.
Find the ones playing with the big balls.
Are any children playing with red balls?
Which children use big red balls?
2

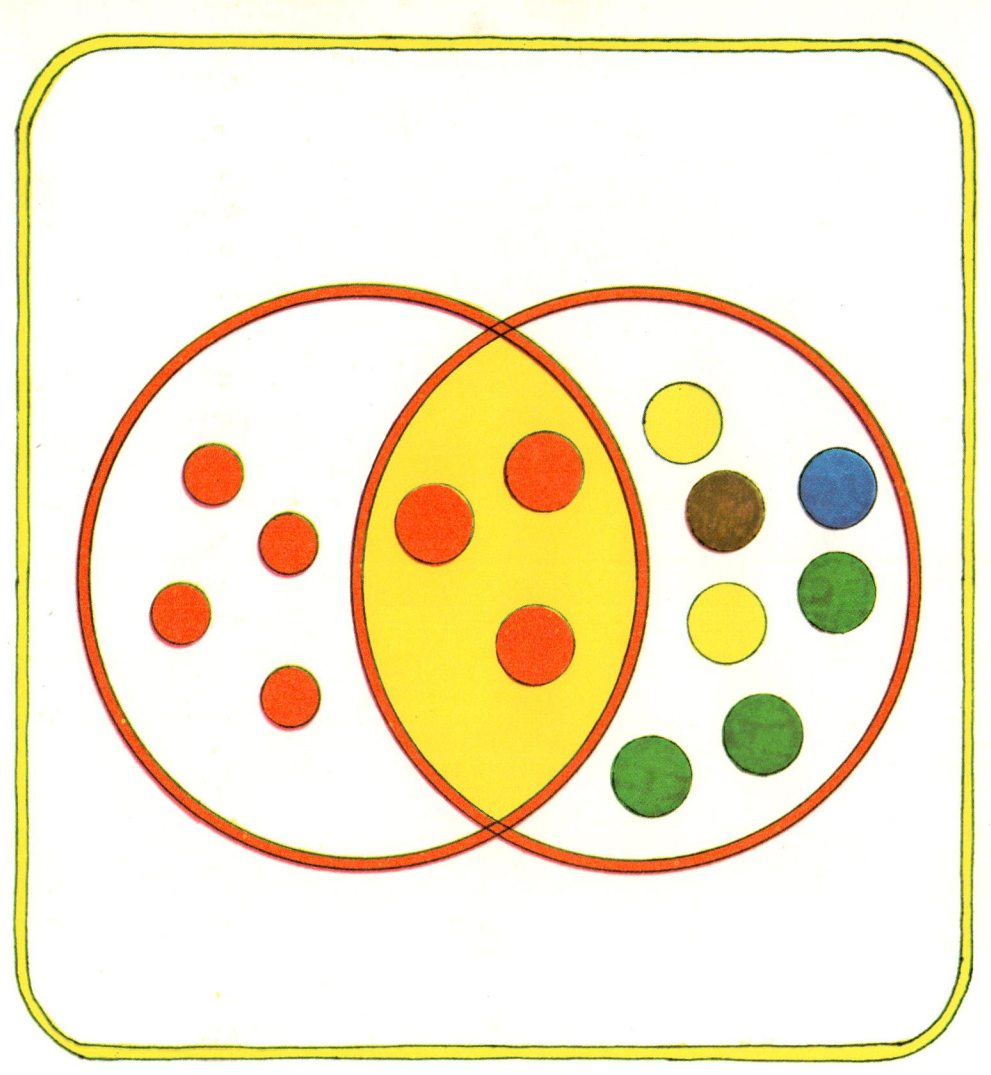

How many of the balls are red?
How many of them are big?
How many are both big and red?

3

Children play in the park.
Which plaything moves round and round?
Which moves up and down?
Which set of things does not move at all?

4

Look at the things moving round.
What shape do they make?
What is the movement of the see-saw?
How does the swing move?

Count the children like this:
first, second, third, and so on.
Which is the fifth child?
Are they in order of size?
6

How many children wait to use the slide?
How many are on the slide?
Will it take them longer to climb up
or to slide down?

The 3 small children
balance the 2 big children.
Could 2 small children
balance 2 big children?
8

The parents push the swings.
They use force when they push.
Is force being used
on the other things?

Look at the shapes in the park.
Can you find the round shapes?
Are there any other shapes you can see?
10

These shapes are painted on the ground.
Look for the shapes which have 4 lines.
How many have 3 lines?
Can you find a shape with one line?

Can you see how the swing moves?
The pendulum on a clock swings
from side to side.
Can you make a pendulum?

12

All these things in the park move.
They move at different speeds.
Which are fast and which are slow?
Try to move in time with moving things.

13

These people belong to a set.
Can you say what the set is?
Do you know what game each plays?
14

These drawings show
what games the people play.
Instead of a football
we can draw a circle.
What games do the other shapes show?

15

The football team is being photographed.
Then they start the football match.
Are they in the same order as before?
How many players are in each picture?

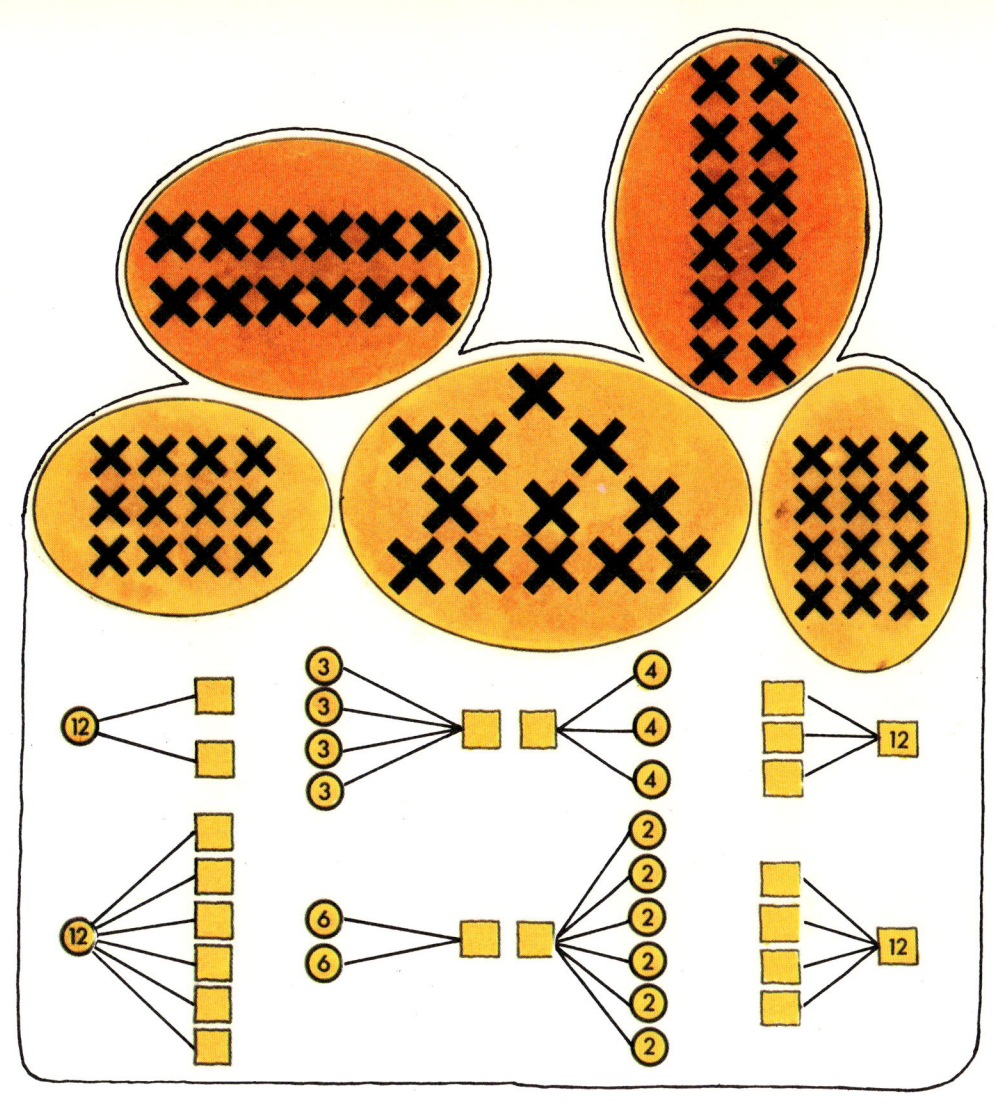

What numbers go in the squares?

The children move in different ways.
They make patterns with their bodies.
Can you make different movements?
What sort of patterns can you make?

18

Some children are pushing things.
Wheels help us move things easily.
What patterns do bouncing balls make?

19

The girl is on the second rung.
She will climb five more rungs.
What number will she be on then?

add 5

2 ⟶ 7

add 5

4 ⟶ ☐

Count the 5's from the first square:
5, 10, 15 . . .
Count in 5's from the second square:
6, 11, 16 . . .

These children measure the playground.
They use ropes, sticks and trundle wheels.
Some measure the lengths in metres.

Here is the 50 metre race.
A man times it with a watch.
How long does it take you to run
50 metres, and how long to walk it?

One boy is throwing a boomerang.
What pattern does it make?
Others fly toy planes.
What pattern will they make?

24

The boy's kite is high in the sky.
What shape is made from boy to kite
to ground?

How many sides has the kite?
How many sides have the other shapes?
In what way are they all the same?
In what way are they different?

The park is closing.
The children have been there for hours.
Can you see what time it is?
How else can you tell that it is late?

Index

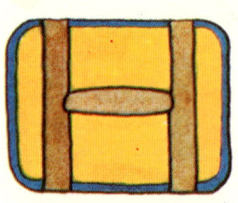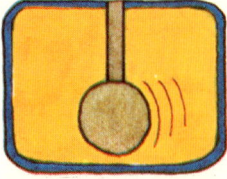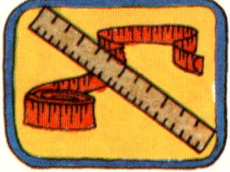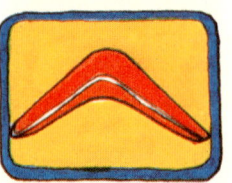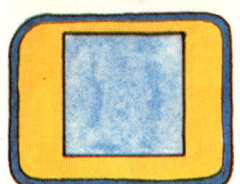